Myths and Civilization of the
ANCIENT
ROMANS

Published in the United States in 1999
by PETER BEDRICK BOOKS
A division of NTC/Contemporary Publishing Group, Inc.
4255 West Touhy Avenue, Lincolnwood (Chicago), Illinois
60646-1975 U.S.A.

The Myths & Civilization series
was created and produced by McRae Books,
via de' Rustici, 5 – Florence, Italy

Editors Anne McRae, Ronne Randall
Illustrations Francesca D'Ottavi (myths), Ivan Stalio,
Alessandro Cantucci, Andrea Morandi (civilization)
Graphic Design Marco Nardi
Cutouts Adriano Nardi, Ornella Fassio
Color separations Litocolor., Florence (Italy)

Printed and bound in Italy by Grafiche Editoriali Padane, Cremona
International Standard Book Number: 0-87226-590-0

99 00 01 02 03 15 14 13 12 11 10 9 8 7 6 5 4 3 2 1

Myths and Civilization of the

ANCIENT ROMANS

John Malam

Illustrations by
Francesca D'Ottavi
Studio Stalio
(Alessandro Cantucci, Fabiano Fabbrucci,
Sauro Giampaia, Andrea Morandi)

PETER BEDRICK BOOKS
NEW YORK

CONTENTS

INTRODUCTION

The civilization of the Romans spanned more than 1,000 years. From modest beginnings in a region of northern Italy, the empire of the Romans spread out to cover many parts of Europe, North Africa, and the Middle East. Within this vast area lived millions of people who came under Roman rule. Some had been conquered in battle by the Roman army; others had accepted the Romans without a struggle. The Romans spread their culture far and wide. Roman coins made in Britain or France could be spent in Spain and Greece, Israel and Egypt. The Roman language, Latin, became the first international tongue – just as English is today. It was in Latin that the myths of the Romans were first spoken and written, telling tales about the history of the Roman people, and of Rome – the city that was the heart and soul of the Roman world.

A myth is a story. It can be about the gods and their powers, the adventures of heroes, fabulous beasts, or strange places where mortal humans cannot go. In the ancient world, the Mesopotamians, Egyptians, and Greeks all told stories like these. The Romans told myths too – but most were not like the myths told in other lands. This was because many Roman myths told stories about ordinary people. The Romans believed their myths told them about themselves, especially about their own history. In this book we explore Roman mythology and civilization. By combining the two, we show how a knowledge of Roman myths provides a basis for understanding Roman society.

HOW THIS BOOK WORKS

This book is divided into sections. Each section starts with a Roman myth, strikingly illustrated on a black background. After each myth comes a double-page information section that looks at an aspect of Roman culture and society, such as daily life, religion, or warfare.

The myth about the twins Romulus and Remus, and how Romulus built a fine city, leads into a nonfiction section about the city of Rome.

Aeneas, the Father of the Romans

Long ago, the citizens of Rome told a story about a warrior from the east who came to live in the land of the Romans. His name was Aeneas, and for them he was the father of the Romans.

The story of Aeneas begins when the goddess Aphrodite came to Earth. She visited Phrygia, that part of the world where Turkey is now, and where the city of Troy once stood. Aphrodite walked among the human race and fell in love with King Anchises.

She bore him a son, whom they called Aeneas. The young Aeneas was cared for by nymphs, but when he was five years old Aphrodite took him away and gave him to his father. Overcome with joy, Anchises boasted that Aphrodite was the mother of his son. On hearing this, Zeus, the ruler of all gods, grew angry. He threw a thunderbolt at Anchises, striking him on the leg and making him lame.

There came a time of war, when soldiers from Greek cities attacked Troy. After ten years of fighting, Troy fell to the Greeks. They invaded the city and set it on fire. Aeneas knew this was the end – there was nothing he could do to save the city. Carrying his aged father on his back, and his young son in his arms, Aeneas escaped to the safety of nearby mountains. For many months they lived there with other survivors from Troy. They built ships, and when the time was right Aeneas led his fellow Trojans in search of a new home.

From Phrygia, Aeneas set sail with a fleet of twenty ships. He stopped at many islands, and on one a fortune-teller made a strange prediction. He told Aeneas he would be at home only when he was so hungry he ate the plate his food came on.

After a long voyage, Aeneas and his ships reached Sicily. But for old Anchises, the journey ended there. He died and was buried on the island. The final part of Aeneas's travels took him to Italy, where on the banks of the River Tiber he shared a meal with the rest of the Trojans. Such was their hunger that they ate the thin loaves of bread they were using as plates. The prediction had come true, and Aeneas knew he was home at last.

Aeneas was in the region known as Latium, the homeland of the Latins. He married the daughter of their king so that the Trojans and Latins were united as one people. Centuries later, when the city of Rome was founded in Latium, its citizens traced their family trees back to Aeneas the Trojan.

Origins

Italy is a country in the south of Europe. It is a peninsula, which means it is almost completely surrounded by sea. About 2,500 years ago, groups of people settled here. One group built their villages on a fertile plain along the west coast of central Italy. They were the Latins, whose cluster of hilltop villages grew into the city of Rome. In later years the Romans told a story about the founding of Rome in which they said the city began in 753 BC. Rome became the greatest city of the ancient world, ruling an empire which spanned Europe and reached as far as the Middle East and Africa.

The Villanovans lived in northern Italy before the Romans. They made metal objects, such as this incense burner.

The Etruscans

The Etruscans lived in the region of Etruria, where they settled in about 800 BC. They were cultured, civilized people, and the Romans learned much from them. The alphabet came to the Romans from the Etruscans, as did gladiator fights, chariot races, and some gods. For a time they were the most powerful people in central Italy, but from the 500s BC onward their power gradually slipped away.

The birth of the city of Rome
Rome began as a village of huts, built on top of a hill. The hill, which later became known as the Palatine Hill, was one of several hills close to the River Tiber. The first huts, belonging to farmers and shepherds, appeared on the Palatine Hill around 1000 BC. Other villages were built on the nearby hills. By about 750 BC the villages had joined together to make a town, and this marked the birth of Rome.

Etruscan warriors wore helmets with high crests, and carried javelins and round shields.

The coast of North Africa, where Tunisia is today, was the home of the Carthaginians. They were seafaring traders, who clashed with both the Greeks and the Romans. Their capital was Carthage.

From monarchy to republic

Rome was at the center of a region called Latium. The inhabitants of the region were the Latins. To the north were the Etruscans, who took control of Rome and ruled there for 100 years. Under the Etruscans, Rome was ruled by kings. The town grew into a city, but the Latins were unhappy at being ruled by cruel "foreign" kings. In 510 BC, the Latins rebelled and threw the Etruscans out. From then on, Rome was a republic, ruled by a group of its leading citizens.

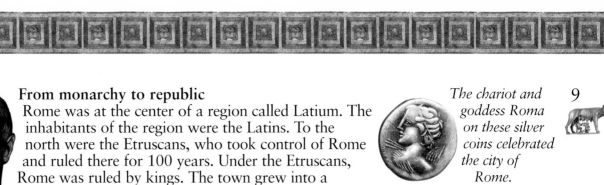

The chariot and goddess Roma on these silver coins celebrated the city of Rome.

Officials called consuls, such as Lucius Junius Brutus seen here, governed Rome during the time of the Republic.

Settlers from Greece lived in southern Italy and Sicily. They brought with them knowledge about science, art, politics, and education. The knowledge of the Greeks was passed on to the Romans. This is a Roman copy of a Greek statue.

THE CONQUEST OF ITALY
(until 264 BC)

CORSICA

SARDINIA

Conquered by 298 BC

Rome

Conquered by 264 BC

MEDITERRANEAN SEA

SICILY

The birth of an empire

In 146 BC the Romans destroyed Carthage and became a world power. Over the next 100 years Rome took control of land from Spain and France in the west, to Greece and Syria in the east. Then, army generals fought a war as to which of them should rule this great empire. It was won by Octavian, who became the first Roman emperor, in 27 BC. He was given the title Augustus, meaning "sacred."

After the expulsion of the Etruscans, the Romans began to take control of all Italy. This man is a Samnite warrior, whose people were defeated by the Romans.

In 218 BC, an army from Carthage, led by Hannibal, invaded Italy. After losing several battles, the Romans forced Hannibal back to Carthage, where he was defeated in 202 BC.

THE WOLF AND THE TWINS

Rome was a wonder to behold, the greatest city the world had ever known. A million people lived there – Romans, foreigners, and slaves. Within its walls were seven hills, the most important of which was the Palatine Hill. The Romans believed that this hill was where the city of Rome had begun.

A long time before Rome's first building stones were laid, there lived a cruel and unkind man called Amulius. His older brother, Numitor, was the king of a city in Latium. After a violent struggle, Amulius overthrew Numitor and made himself king. Then he turned on Numitor's family, killing his sons and forbidding his daughter, Rhea Silvia, from having children. Amulius did these terrible things to prevent Numitor from having descendants who might one day seek their revenge. Amulius was sure his plan would succeed. When Rhea Silvia gave birth to twin boys, whose father was the god Mars, Amulius ordered that they should be drowned in the River Tiber. His servants took the babies, whose names were Romulus and Remus, and placed them in a basket. But they were too kind-hearted to carry out Amulius's orders, and so they left the basket to float away to safety.

It came to rest beside a fig tree, where it was found by a she-wolf who had heard the babies' cries. She fed them with her own milk, and a woodpecker gave them scraps of food. When a shepherd saw this, he knew at once who the babies were. He took them home to his wife, and they raised them as their own sons.

Romulus and Remus grew into fine young men. One day, the shepherd met Numitor, and told him that his grandsons were alive and well. When Romulus and Remus learned who they really were, they sought revenge against Amulius. He was killed, and Numitor was king once more.

The brothers now decided to build a city of their own. They chose a place on the banks of the River Tiber, close to where they had been left to die as infants. But they quarreled as to who should name the city and become its king. Since they did not know which twin was the elder, they left it to the gods to send a sign. They stood on separate hills, and looked to the heavens. Remus saw six vultures, but Romulus saw twelve. Each believed the gods had meant him to be king – Remus because he saw the birds first, Romulus because he had seen the most.

A fight began, and Romulus killed his brother. By himself Romulus built the city on the hill which the Romans later called the Palatine Hill. He named the city Rome, after himself.

The City of Rome

Rome's first emperor, Augustus (reigned BC 27 to AD 14), said of the city: "I inherited it brick and left it marble." It was his way of saying that he had given fine new buildings to Rome. Emperors who came later left their mark on the city too, such as Vespasian (reigned ad 69 to 79), who built the Flavian Amphitheater, known in later times as the Colosseum. It was a massive oval-shaped arena, used for public games and gladiatorial contests.

Roma, whose name means "strength," was the goddess of Rome. The city was named after her.

A huge cloth could be drawn across for shade.

Women sat in the wooden seats at the top.

Gladiators fought on the sand-covered center.

Seats for 50,000 people.

The Colosseum
This cutaway reconstruction shows the tiers of seating and the arena.

Rome in the AD 300s, surrounded by a 32-mile long wall.

This bronze figure of a she-wolf suckling the twins Romulus and Remus was made in about 500 BC. Pieces of art, like this, reminded Romans about their past.

The Roman Forum

All roads in Rome converged on one small square in the city center. This was the Roman Forum. It was the commercial, political, religious, and social center of the Roman world. Surrounding the square were many temples and public buildings, where decisions about governing the city and the empire were made. Rome's citizens gathered in the Forum to hear politicians speak, triumphant generals marched through it, sacrifices were made here, and bankers, money-lenders, and food sellers conducted their business in nearby arcades.

The Baths of Caracalla

The Baths of Caracalla, completed in AD 216, was a vast complex of libraries, gardens, gyms, and pools, where 1,600 people at a time could bathe, exercise, talk, and relax.

Rome's buildings

By the time of Emperor Constantine (reigned 307 to 337) Rome had 28 libraries, 8 bridges, 11 public baths, 2 circuses, 2 amphitheaters, 290 warehouses, 1,352 fountains, 144 public lavatories, 46,602 apartments, 1,797 private houses, and a population of about 1.5 million.

Reconstruction of the Baths of Caracalla.

In 204 BC Rome was at war with Carthage, a city on the north coast of Africa. The Carthaginian army had invaded Italy, and the Romans were desperate to find a way to drive the foreigners from their land.

Rome's leaders consulted the Sibylline Books – a collection of prophecies. They guided the Romans in times of trouble, and in the war with Carthage a prophecy told them how to defeat their enemy. It said: "The mother is absent. You must find her. When she comes, she must be received by honest hands."

The Romans were puzzled, and a group of them went to the oracle, or fortune-teller, at Delphi, in Greece, for more information. There they were told to: "Fetch the Great Mother who lives on Mount Ida." Now they knew what they must do to save Rome, for they knew that the Great Mother was none other than the goddess Cybele, the Mother of the Gods. Her symbol on Earth was a sacred stone, and just as the oracle had said, it was on Mount Ida, in the land of Phrygia. The Romans had to take the stone to Rome.

With the stone on board their ship, the Romans sailed back to Rome. But as their journey neared its end, disaster struck. As the ship entered the mouth of the River Tiber, it became stuck on a sandbank.

Strong men pulled on ropes tied to the ship, but it would not move. People grew worried that the goddess Cybele was unhappy. Perhaps this was an omen that Rome would lose the war. Then a woman called Claudia Quinta, who had been wrongly accused of a crime she had not committed, prayed to Cybele. With arms held high, Claudia prayed that Cybele would send a sign to prove she was innocent.

Then Claudia gently pulled on one of the ropes tied to the ship and, miraculously, it moved as easily as if it was a toy. This sign from heaven proved Claudia's innocence. Freed from the sandbank, the ship sailed into port.

Just as the prophecy had forecast, the Great Mother had been received by honest hands, and now that the sacred stone was in Rome, the Romans knew they would soon win the war.

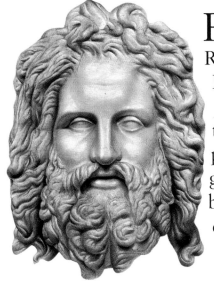

Religion

Roman religion grew from an ancient belief in spirits. It was the spirits who guided people's lives. As time passed, the spirits became the gods and goddesses of the Romans. Each one had special powers. In some parts of the Roman world people believed in other gods. When the religion of the Christians, who believed in only one true god, reached Rome, it spread quickly and replaced the gods of old.

Chief god of the Romans was Jupiter. He was god of sky, daylight, and weather.

Some temples grew into large complexes, with courtyards surrounded by colonnades.

Roman temples

A temple was a house for a god. Inside was a statue of the god. Worshipers believed the god lived within the statue. It faced the door so it could "see," the courtyard outside. At an altar in the courtyard, sheep were sacrificed and gifts were left to please the god.

Bacchus was the god of wine. His followers held wild, drunken parties, dancing and calling out to him.

Sabazius was a god of creation from the east. His sign, a raised hand, was adopted by early Christians in Rome.

Superstition

Superstition played a great part in the lives of many Romans. Astrologers studied the stars to predict the future. Sorceresses – who were like witches – mixed potions to bring good luck or bad luck. Ordinary people wrote curses to harm others, and there was widespread belief in ghosts and evil. It was bad luck to fall over in the street or to hear an owl hoot – but it was good luck to see bees and snakes.

RECONSTRUCTION OF THE TEMPLE OF FORTUNA PRENESTINA, NEAR ROME.

After AD 313, Christians could openly worship their god. At first they met in houses, but soon churches were built, like this one.

Peter and Paul were Christians who took Christianity to the Romans. Both were executed in Rome.

Mystery cults from the east

The Romans came into contact with many religions different from their own. Some became popular with the Romans, such as mystery cults from the east. At secret ceremonies followers went into trances. They felt close to their god.

Isis, a goddess from Egypt, was worshiped by some Romans. Followers of her cult believed in life after death. In their ceremonies they sang hymns, read from sacred books, and shook rattles.

Christianity

Christianity was an eastern religion which came to Rome in the AD 40s. Unlike the Roman religion which had many gods, Christians worshiped only one god. They believed they were favored people, blessed with the promise of eternal life. For almost 300 years the Romans persecuted the Christians, who were forced to meet in secret.

By spilling the blood of a bull, the eastern god Mithras gave life to all living things.

GREEK GODS INTO ROMAN GODS

The Romans learned many things from their neighbors, the Greeks. The Greeks had gods who they believed controlled nature and people's lives. The Romans adopted many of these gods and worshiped them as their own. They gave them Roman names. For example, Zeus, the chief Greek god, became Jupiter, and Hera, his wife, became Juno.

Religion in the home

In their daily lives, the Romans believed they were constantly watched over by spirits. Some spirits, called lares, protected the home. At the start of each new day the family said prayers at the household shrine, or lararium, like the one seen here. Small gifts of food were left at the shrine, to please the spirits and ask for their protection.

The Sacred Fire of Rome

Long before Rome became a great city, it was a small hill village. Inside each crudely built house was a hearth where a fire burned. There was no chimney, and smoke was left to find its way out through gaps in the walls and roof. Fires were kept permanently alight in people's homes as an act of worship to the gods: a cold hearth meant an empty, godless house. Rome's first fire, said the Romans, had been lit from a spark brought by Aeneas from the faraway city of Troy. Aeneas, the father of the Romans, had carried the sacred fire of Troy across seas and mountains, and it was his gift to the people of Rome.

As the years passed, the village grew. There were other villages on nearby hills, and they grew too, until eventually they came together to make a town. From that town came the city of Rome.

Rome was a magnificent city. At its center was the Forum, a large area filled with temples, arches, columns, and statues. From one of the temples a plume of smoke drifted into the sky. This was the Temple of Vesta, built in honor of the goddess of the hearth. It was a small temple and, unlike the others, it was round. It was built that way to remind Romans of the first houses and the city's humble beginnings.

A fire was kept constantly alight inside the Temple of Vesta, just like the fires that had burned inside Rome's first houses. It was the sacred fire of Rome. If it died, Rome would be in danger.

Near the temple was the House of Vesta. It was the home of six priestesses called Vestal Virgins. They became priestesses while still children, between the ages of six and ten, and then served the temple for thirty years. Their main duty was to keep the temple fire burning day and night, never letting it go out. But there were occasions when storms raged and drafts blew the fire out. When this happened, the Vestals were accused of neglecting their duties, and they were flogged. Some, however, escaped this punishment by performing miracles. Take, for example, the priestess Aemilia, who was accused of allowing the fire to die. As her accusers watched, she prayed to the goddess Vesta to send a sign to prove she was innocent of the crime. Aemilia ripped a piece of linen from her dress and threw it onto the fire's cold ashes. A wisp of gray smoke curled up from the cloth. Then, out of the smoke came fire. Rome's sacred fire burned bright once more, the city was safe, and Aemilia was spared from punishment.

Emperor and State

During the Roman Empire the head of state was the emperor. He was the supreme ruler of the Roman world. As Rome's influence spread out from Italy, the Roman Empire was formed. It reached its greatest extent during the reign of Trajan (reigned AD 98 to 117), when as many as 50 million people lived within its many parts, called provinces. The Romans wanted to take their ideas about civilization to the edges of the world. In return, the provinces sent food, slaves and other goods to Rome.

Julius Caesar (lived 100 to 44 BC) became the most powerful man in Rome.

Citizens of Rome

Only men counted as Roman citizens – those born to Roman citizens (the freeborn), those freed from slavery (freedmen), and those granted citizenship by the state. Men in all parts of the Empire could be citizens of Rome. They were protected by Roman law, and got state aid, such as free grain.

The Vestal Virgins kept Rome's sacred fire alight. If it went out, Rome would face danger.

An eagle was the state's symbol of power.

EMPERORS AS DIVINE BEINGS

After Julius Caesar's murder in 44 BC, people began to think about him as if he was a god. This fact made a difference to the emperors who ruled the Roman Empire. Caesar's adopted son, Octavian, was the first Roman emperor (he used the name Augustus). Because Caesar was a god, therefore Augustus was the son of a god – and so most emperors were thought of as gods living on Earth for people to worship as divine beings.

An emperor's life

Marcus Aurelius (reigned AD 161 to 180), seen here on horseback, was thought of as the perfect emperor. He was a thoughtful man, devoted to his public duties to serve the people and protect the Empire. He kept a diary in which he wrote his thoughts about his life as emperor.

Augustus, the first Roman emperor
In 27 BC, Augustus became the first emperor, and the period known as the Roman Empire began. His reign was marked by peace, order and good government. It was a time when new buildings were built in Rome. He was short, was married three times, and had one child, a girl.

THE ROMAN EMPIRE
AT ITS GREATEST EXTENT

Roman soldiers in the provinces not only protected the frontiers of the Empire. They also farmed the land, built roads and bridges and generally helped spread Roman culture into the newly conquered areas.

BRITAIN

GAUL

ITALY

SPAIN

GREECE

TURKEY

NORTH AFRICA

MEDITERRANEAN SEA

EGYPT

Feeding Rome's poor
In the mosaic above, a state official is handing grain to Rome's poorest citizens. The "corn dole" prevented poverty and starvation, made work for people in the city's warehouses, and ensured that the poor – about 200,000 in total – would support the government.

Even after 2,000 years, many fine examples of Roman architecture survive, such as this aqueduct in North Africa that carried drinking water to a city.

THE SLAVE GIRLS SAVE THE CITY

In 390 BC Rome was looted by the Gauls, who came from uncivilized lands to the north. The Gauls stayed in Rome for many months, and only left after they were given a large amount of gold.

With the barbarians gone, the Romans expected life to return to normal. But they were mistaken. Rome had been weakened by the Gauls, and after they left a second attack was made against the city.

This time, Rome was attacked by the Latins – the people in whose territory Rome was built. The army of the Latins camped outside Rome, and ambassadors were sent into the city with a message. It said: "Send us your daughters to be our brides, for we wish the Latins and the Romans to be brought closer together." When the message was read out, there was panic in the streets, and for a while no one knew what to do. Then a slave girl, whose name was Philotis, came forward. She had an idea.

Philotis said she and other young slave girls should go to the Latins and pretend to be freeborn Roman women. Then, at night, she would signal to the Romans that they could attack their enemy while they lay in their beds. The Romans listened as Philotis explained her plan. All agreed it was their only hope to save Rome from disaster.

Philotis and her fellow slave girls were given fine clothes and gold jewelry to wear, and dressed as brides they went into the camp of the Latins. Once inside they told the Latins that it was a special day for the Romans too. They said it was a festival day, when Romans drank, ate, and enjoyed themselves. In the feast that followed, the slave girls served the Latins with food and drink. The Latins, who were soon drunk, fell into a deep sleep. While the girls

hid the Latins' swords, Philotis climbed a fig tree and waved a burning torch. This was the signal, and an army of Roman soldiers left Rome and headed toward the Latins' camp. Unseen, they crept into the camp and slaughtered the Latins as they slept.

Rome was safe, and every year thereafter, on July 7, a feast was held to honor Philotis and the other girls. Called the "Feast of the Fig Tree," it was a day when female servants were allowed to do as they pleased, and when Romans remembered how their city had been saved by the bravery of the slave girls.

Food, Feasts, and Entertainment

Farmers were the backbone of Roman society. They grew the food that went to market to feed the people who lived in towns. It was in towns where life was lived to the full. Visitors from near and far came to be entertained, enjoying an afternoon watching a play in an open-air theater, the thrills and spills of chariot racing, or the drama of the games in the arena. And afterward, there might be a meal: a banquet in the house of a wealthy Roman, or, for the poor, something cheap and simple in one of the town's many taverns.

In the arena, men called gladiators fought with swords, spears and tridents. Some wore helmets like this one and armor.

A Roman marriage
The Romans had arranged marriages, where fathers chose husbands for their daughters. Marriage marked the passing of a girl to her husband. Her husband took charge of her from then on. At the ceremony, the bride, dressed in white, was aided by a matron of honor. The couple signed a contract, joined hands, and said their vows.

Chariots raced at a track called a "circus." The best horses came from Spain.

Skilled craftworkers
The Romans had many crafts. They made objects out of stone, clay, glass, metal, wood, bone, ivory and leather.

Public entertainment
When a town staged its games, people flocked to the local arena to watch gladiators fight each other or wild beasts. Elsewhere in town, charioteers raced at great speed around a racetrack, drawn by two, three, or four horses, while at the theater tragic or comic plays were staged.

Glass was a luxury only the rich could afford. The poor used cheaper vessels made from pottery.

At the theater, actors wore masks to show if they were sad or happy.

When the wheat harvest was gathered, the grains of grain were taken to a mill, like the one here. Water from a river or stream was channeled to the mill, where it was emptied over a water wheel. As the force of the falling water turned the wheel, it made power to turn grindstones. Grain was crushed between the stones, and flour was made.

The best wheat made very white flour.

Bakers used flour to make bread and pastries. Some people baked their own at home.

Wheat was crushed to make flour, which was used for baking or mixed with water to make porridge.

Food of the poor
The poor made do with puls, which was a thick, sticky porridge or gruel made from cereal grains. They drank cheap wine, diluted with water.

Figs were a popular fresh fruit, eaten at meals.

Grapes made wine, which everyone drank.

Olives gave oil for cooking. They were also eaten fresh or pickled.

Food of the rich
Wealthy Romans held lavish banquets. Guests lay on couches and ate with their fingers. A feast lasted several hours, starting with shellfish, snails and eggs, then roast meat, sauces, and cabbage, and finishing with fruit, nuts, and pastries. Wine and water were drunk with each course.

FESTIVALS
Festivals were held on many days throughout the Roman year. They were public holidays, when people enjoyed themselves and gave thanks to the gods. A lot of festivals were linked to the seasons and marked important dates in the farming year. For example, at the festival of Fordicidia (April 15), cattle were sacrificed to ensure that the soil would bear good crops, and at the festival of Vestalia (June 9) storehouses were cleaned in preparation for the grain from the harvest.

THE BATTLE OF THE CHAMPIONS

In the early days of Rome, the nearby city of Alba Longa was its rival. It too wanted to be the region's leading city, and its people, the Albans, thought they should be the masters of Rome. But while the Romans and the Albans quarreled, they both knew their real enemy was across the River Tiber in Etruria. This was where the Etruscans lived, an old and powerful people who had lived in Italy far longer than either the Romans or the Albans.

The Roman and Alban leaders knew that if their armies fought each other, both sides would be weakened. It would leave them open to attack from the Etruscans, who would surely be the winners. And so the Romans and the Albans decided on a plan to settle their differences.

Each side chose a set of identical triplets to fight for them. The three Horatius brothers would fight for Rome, and the Curatius brothers would represent the Albans. It would be the Battle of the Champions, the fight to end all fights.

Clad in armor and brandishing swords, the Roman three attacked the Alban triplets. Before long, the Albans were wounded, and two of the Romans lay dead. The third, whose name was Publius Horatius, fled from the battlefield.

Onlookers watched as the three Albans chased Horatius. But Horatius was cunning. He was not running away out of fear, but because he knew the Albans were injured and their wounds would slow them down. Sure enough, the wounded Albans chased Horatius at different speeds, and he was able to turn and kill them one by one.

Horatius was declared the champion of champions, and Rome was proclaimed the supreme city. In recognition of his great deed, Horatius was awarded the cloaks and swords of the fallen Albans.

In Rome, Horatius was greeted as a hero. But when his sister met him she burst into tears. Only then did Horatius discover that she had been engaged to one of the Albans he had killed. Overcome with rage, Horatius plunged his sword into her heart crying: "So perish all Roman women who mourn a foe!"

By this terrible act, Horatius had taken the law into his own hands. He stood trial and was sentenced to death by hanging. But the Roman people could not bring themselves to execute their hero, and so Horatius, the man who had single-handedly defeated the Albans, was set free.

The Roman Army

The Romans faced many enemies. At first it was their neighbors in Italy, such as the Etruscans and Samnites. As Rome began to form an empire, carved from other lands, wars were fought against foreign nations. The army built parts of the Empire by conquest. But later, the army's job changed to defending the Empire's frontiers. During the AD 400s, the frontiers were crossed by barbarian tribes. The Roman army tried to push them back, but in the end the barbarians proved too strong for the Romans.

The only soldiers permanently stationed in Rome were the 10,000 men of the Praetorian Guard. Their job was to defend the city and the emperor.

A fort was a soldiers' village. Supplies and troops came in by road.

Roman forts – the outposts of empire
Forts were built throughout the Roman Empire. Some were temporary marching camps, surrounded by ditches and banks of earth. Others were permanent settlements protected by stone walls. Inside were barrack buildings where the soldiers slept and ate, bathhouses, toilet blocks, workshops, doctors quarters, granaries, and stables.

A soldier's short sword, called a "gladius," and its scabbard. It was a slashing weapon.

A soldier's metal helmet protected the head and neck.

Forts could be protected by steep-sided ditches, iron spikes rammed into the ground, and pointed wooden stakes.

Organization of the army

During the Roman Empire, the army had about thirty large units called legions. Each legion had some 5,000 foot soldiers or legionaries, and a small number of horsemen. Legionaries were divided into ten groups called cohorts, with about 500 men in each. Cohorts were made up of small units, called centuries, with about 80 men in each. A century was under the command of a centurion.

Siege towers with battering rams were used to knock down the enemy's wall.

Several types of heavy artillery machinery were used to weaken an enemy. Catapults shot big arrows tipped with iron or burning rags, and other machines hurled heavy rocks over long distances.

A pole, called a standard, was carried into battle. To lose it was a disgrace to the legion.

By raising shields above their heads, soldiers formed a "testudo," or tortoise. It protected them from stones and arrows.

Battle tactics

Battles were usually planned long in advance. Scouts spied on an enemy and reported on their numbers and weapons. This gave the Roman generals time to decide the best way to mount an attack. Sometimes a town or stronghold was besieged. The army camped outside for weeks or months, waiting for the people inside to give in – or die of hunger.

Some of Rome's enemies fought with elephants, shooting arrows from towers on their backs.

THE RAPE OF LUCRETIA

In the days when Rome was ruled by an unpopular family of kings called the Tarquins, the Romans were at war with the nearby city of Ardea. One day, during a long siege, a Roman general called Collatinus fell into conversation with other commanders. They talked about their wives at home in Rome, and which of them was leading the most virtuous life.

Collatinus said that his wife, Lucretia, would win the contest. The others disagreed, and to solve the argument they rode to Rome to visit their wives by surprise. This way they would discover who was leading the most virtuous life.

The men went to their homes at night. All of the women, except one, were enjoying themselves at elegant dinner parties. Their husbands were shocked. But when Collatinus visited Lucretia, he found her at work with her maid-servants, spinning wool. She alone had lived up to everything her husband had claimed for her.

But Lucretia was more than just well-behaved. Men were struck by her great beauty, and one, Sextus Tarquinius, who had ridden to Rome with her husband, fell in love with her. He was a Tarquin, son of the king. A few days later Tarquinius returned secretly to Lucretia's house, where he was greeted as an honored guest. He told Lucretia he had fallen in love with her. Lucretia would not hear of it. Tarquinius was determined to get his own way, and so he threatened to kill Lucretia and a slave. Lucretia was faced with a terrible choice: whether to give in to Tarquinius or die. Either way, her fate was sealed, and she gave in to the vile demands of Tarquinius.

After Tarquinius had left, Lucretia summoned her father and her husband. Each brought a friend. The four men listened to Lucretia's story. They did their best to comfort her, saying she should not feel guilty since it was Tarquinius who had forced himself upon her. Lucretia felt her honor had been taken from her. She picked up a knife and stabbed herself through the heart. As for Tarquinius, he did not get away with his crime. When the people heard what he had done they rose up against the Tarquins and overthrew the monarchy. From then on Rome was a republic, no longer ruled by kings, but by men chosen by the people. For this, Lucretia was forever remembered as the woman who gave the Romans their freedom from tyrants.

Daily Life

Within a few minutes of waking up at dawn, Roman men and women were dressed and ready to begin the day. In wealthy families men went to the barber, while servants helped women to arrange their hair and jewelry. As the day progressed, there might be visits to the arena, theater, or the baths, before the evening meal at home, followed by bed for the night.

Roman mother and her servant bathing a child.

Emperor Septimus Severus (reigned AD 193 to 211), his wife Julia Domna, and their sons Geta and Caracalla. Geta, whose portrait is defaced, was murdered by Caracalla.

The importance of the family

Families were important in Roman society. To the Romans, the word *familia* meant a father, mother, and their children, together with their slaves and close relatives. The father was the head of the family and the household. He set a good example for his sons to follow, since they would lead the family after his death.

A woman gathering wild flowers. This scene was painted on the wall of a house.

Apartment buildings at Ostia housed Rome's growing population.

Women in Roman society

It was a woman's duty to care for the family and the home, cooking, cleaning, looking after the children, and making clothes. If she lived in a wealthy family, she ordered slaves to do the work. But women from poor families had to do this work on their own. Women could not vote, or work in the government.

Houses in towns and in the country

In Roman towns in Italy, the wealthy and their servants lived in private houses. They were single-story buildings, with rooms built around a courtyard. Some had gardens. The poor lived in small, overcrowded apartments in buildings two or three stories high. The dark rooms had no running water or toilets. In the country there were farms, and large houses called villas. Only the rich could afford villas in the country, which they used as "vacation homes," away from towns.

Women's hairstyles

Women paid a lot of attention to their hair, which was always kept long. As fashions changed, different hairstyles were worn. The simplest style was for the hair to be drawn into a knot at the back of the head, where it was held in place with ribbons or pins. Ringlets, curls, and braids were also popular. Some women wore wigs, made with hair brought from Germany, and even from India. A mixture of vinegar and lentil oil was used to dye brown hair blonde.

In the AD 100s it was fashionable for women to wear their hair high at the front with a knot at the back.

Combs were made from ivory, boxwood, and tortoiseshell. This one belonged to a woman called Modestina.

Necklace and ring made from gold and semi-precious stones.

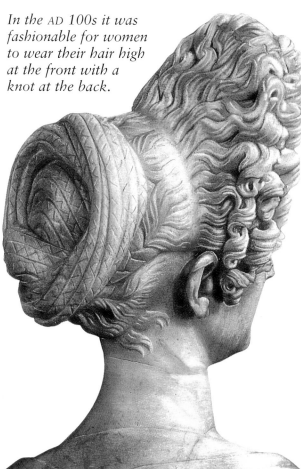

Jewelry

The Romans wore necklaces, rings, chains, bangles, and brooches. There were workshops in Rome, though much jewelry was made in the Middle East, at Alexandria and Antioch, by Greek jewelers. In the early years of Roman history pieces were made from plain gold, but as time went by jewelers added emeralds, sapphires, pearls, and even diamonds to their creations.

Clothes and shoes

For much of Roman history the standard item of clothing for men was the toga. It was a large piece of semicircular woolen cloth, draped loosely from the shoulders. Women wore a long belted gown, called a stola. Both items went out of fashion during the time of the Roman Empire, replaced by simpler tunics decorated with wide stripes. Boots, sandals, and indoor shoes were made of leather. Children wore the same styles as grown-ups.

QUEEN DIDO TRIES TO TRAP AENEAS

Many tales are told about Aeneas and the adventures he had as he sailed from Troy to Italy. Before Aeneas reached Italy, his ships were blown off course by a storm. Many of his faithful sailors were feared drowned. His seven remaining ships, their sails torn and timbers battered, headed to the shelter of an unfamiliar coastline. The coastline was that of north Africa, and Aeneas landed close to the city of Carthage, the home of Queen Dido. Aeneas ordered his crew to stay by their ships and set off toward the city. As he walked through the country, the goddess Venus appeared and told him about the people he would meet. To protect him, the goddess shrouded Aeneas in a mist which made him invisible.

Inside the city's great temple he watched as Queen Dido commanded her people to do her work. And then he saw something which amazed him, for standing in a group were the Trojan sailors he thought had drowned at sea. This was powerful magic indeed, and Queen Dido must surely be a great ruler to pluck men from the teeth of a storm. She listened as the Trojans told of their adventures with Aeneas, and how it was his plan to build a new city to replace Troy.

When Queen Dido said she must find Aeneas, the mist of invisibility that hid the hero from view suddenly lifted. Aeneas was revealed!

That night, at a banquet, Aeneas entertained the queen. She was captivated, not only by the stories she heard, but by Aeneas himself. She was soon in love with him, and began to plan a way of keeping him for herself.

But the gods had other plans for Aeneas, for they knew it was his destiny to sail to Italy. They watched as Queen Dido plotted to marry Aeneas and trap him in Carthage. Aeneas seemed unable to break free from her spell. The gods knew that they must act, and they sent Mercury with a message.

Mercury, the god of travelers and messages, told Aeneas that his future lay in Italy, not with Queen Dido. When Aeneas, who was now free of her magic, told her he was leaving, she pleaded with him to stay. But it was no use. Aeneas knew he must continue on his journey.

Overcome with grief, Queen Dido ordered a fire to be built. She wanted to destroy everything that reminded her of Aeneas. Then, as she watched the Trojans' ships depart, she fell on a sword and died. The fire was lit, and its flames consumed more than just the memories of Aeneas, for it was now Queen Dido's funeral pyre.

As for Aeneas, he never looked back. He sailed to Italy and his future as the father of the Roman people.

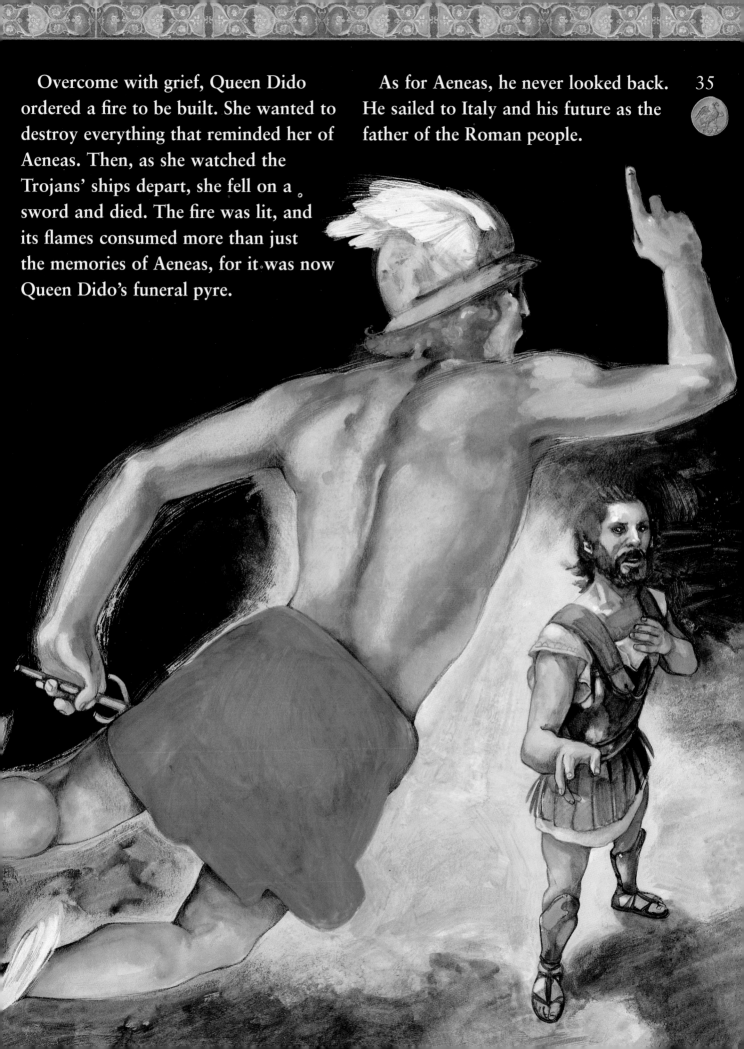

Trade and Transportation

It's true to say that all roads led to – and from – Rome. This was because the Golden Milestone in the center of the city was the starting point for the Empire's roads. The names of towns and their distances from Rome were written on it in gold letters. Roads were not the only means of communication – the sea was just as important. Into Rome's ports came the wealth of her Empire – wines and fruits of Italy; grain and dates of Africa; oil of Spain; meat, wood, and wool of Gaul; marble of Greece; paper of Egypt – all to be sold in the city's busy markets.

Many a ship never reached its destination. Storms, pirates, and rocks took their toll, sending sailors and ships to the bottom of the sea.

In towns, farmers and other traders sold their goods from market stands, as in the scene shown here.

Bankers worked in the marketplace, exchanging foreign currency and lending money.

The Romans traded with people far beyond the limits of their Empire. Silk, spice, and gems came from Asia, ivory from Africa, and incense from the Middle East.

A network of roads

There were about 53,000 miles of roads in the Empire. Many were made by soldiers as the army extended the limits of the Empire. Later on, merchants, couriers, and travelers used them.

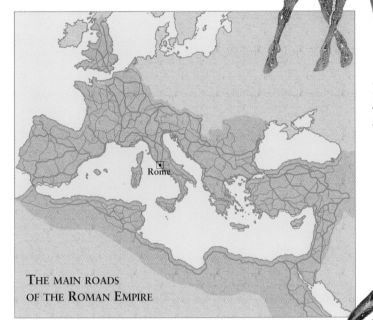

THE MAIN ROADS OF THE ROMAN EMPIRE

The postal system used couriers to carry letters across the Empire, traveling about 50 miles a day.

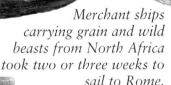

Below, a merchant ship sails into Ostia, one of Romes two main ports. On the right its cargo, such as wine, is enjoyed by customers at a city tavern.

Merchant ships carrying grain and wild beasts from North Africa took two or three weeks to sail to Rome.

A balance for weighing goods. The weight is shaped like a person.

Farmers and merchants used wagons to move their goods along the roads. Travelers went by horse, or on foot. Some main roads had "service stations" where horses could be fed and changed.

Coins and money

Mints – places where coins were made – existed in many towns in the Empire. The coins made there could be used anywhere in the Roman world. They were made of bronze, silver, and gold. Each type of coin had its own name and value.

CASTOR AND POLLUX – THE HEAVENLY TWINS

To the east of Italy is the land of Greece. The Greeks were very wise, and the Romans learned many things from them. When the Romans learned about Zeus and the other gods of the Greeks, they began to worship them as their own. The Romans gave them new names, which is how the Greek god Zeus became the Roman god Jupiter.

The Greeks told stories about their gods. One story was about "Zeus's boys" who were twin brothers called Castor and Polydeuces. The Romans called them Castor and Pollux, and, as time passed, they made up their own stories about the "heavenly twins."

The Romans told how Castor and Pollux helped them win a battle against their neighbors, the Latins. Out of nowhere rode the twins. On white stallions at the head of the Roman cavalry, they charged at the Latins, who were soon defeated. Then, by some strange magic, the twins appeared in the center of Rome, many miles from the battlefield. They watered their horses in a sacred pool, told the crowds about the Roman victory over the Latins, and vanished.

In another story told by the Romans, Castor and Pollux were seen by a man called Publius Vatinius. He was on his way to Rome when he had a vision. It was late at night, and out of the darkness came the heavenly twins, riding along the road.

Their sudden appearance startled Vatinius. But he had nothing to fear, for the twins had good news, saying the Roman army had been victorious against their enemies, the Macedonians.

Vatinius hurried on to Rome and gave the news to the city's leaders. They did not believe him. They thought he was tricking them with lies – why would Castor and Pollux come to Vatinius and not them? Poor old Vatinius was taken away and locked up.

Many weeks later a messenger brought news that the Roman army really had defeated the Macedonians. At once, the people knew that Vatinius had told the truth – Castor and Pollux really had come to him, just as he had said.

Vatinius was set free, and to make amends for the way he had been wronged he was given some land. As for Castor and Pollux, they continued to be worshiped by the Romans, in the temple built in their honor.

Inside houses, paintings in strong colors decorated the walls of rooms. Landscapes were popular, as were scenes from mythology.

Art, Literature, and Science

The Romans were civilized, cultured people. Scientists, doctors, and thinkers explored the world they knew, looking for ways to explain its many secrets. Artists recorded the world they saw in paintings, mosaics, and sculptures. Books, poems, and plays came from the pens of writers, and historians wrote about Rome's origins, emperors, wars, and everyday life. It is from sources such as these that we are able to piece together the Roman world, bringing the past to life.

Pieces of colored marble have been used to make this picture of a tiger attacking an animal.

The art of cameo making was perfected by the Romans. A cameo is a semi-precious stone with a design carved on it in relief. They were used as items of jewelry, and as inlays for furniture, like the ones shown above.

BOOKS AND WRITING

The Romans wrote on papyrus, a type of paper made in Egypt from the stems of water reeds. Many small sheets of papyrus were joined together to make a long strip of paper. This was rolled around a wooden winding stick, and was the Roman version of a book, called a book roll. To write with, pens were made from the quills of birds, feathers, or from pieces of bone. They were dipped into red or black ink. Mistakes could be rubbed out with a damp sponge. Large towns had libraries where book rolls were kept.

Seneca (lived from about 5 BC to AD 65) was a writer, lawyer, and philosopher. He wrote a book in which he poked fun at Emperor Claudius. Its English title is The Pumpkinification of the Divine Claudius – *which was Seneca's way of saying the emperor was turning into a pumpkin!*

Virgil (lived from 70 to 19 BC) is one of the greatest poets of the ancient world. His most famous work, the Aeneid, *is the story of Aeneas, the father of the Roman people. It took eleven years to write.*

Ovid (lived from 43 BC to AD 17) trained as a lawyer, but turned to poetry. His most famous work, Metamorphoses, *is a collection of myths.*

Cicero (lived from 106 to 43 BC) was a politician and writer. He studied law, Greek literature, and oratory – the art of making speeches. Many of his speeches were written down, and they tell us about life in Rome.

The Mosaic

A mosaic is a pattern or a picture made from small pieces of colored stone and glass, called *tesserae*. The pieces were pressed into a bed of wet cement, which set hard. A mosaic surface was hard-wearing and long-lasting. The Romans decorated the floors, walls, and even the ceilings of their buildings with mosaics.

Pliny (lived from AD 23 to 79) was a scholar. As a young man he served in the army where he wrote about throwing missiles from horseback. His greatest work, Natural History, *is an encyclopedia of popular science. He was killed watching the eruption of the volcano Vesuvius, in AD 79.*

Livy (lived from 59 BC to AD 17) was a historian. His greatest work was a collection of 142 books, of which 35 have survived. They are the story of the city of Rome, from its very beginning to the year 9 BC.

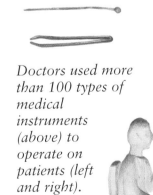

Doctors used more than 100 types of medical instruments (above) to operate on patients (left and right).

Doctors and medicine

Roman doctors performed operations and prescribed medicines, many of which were based on herbal remedies. Garlic was mixed into potions used to treat leprosy, and saffron was useful for eye complaints.

The Fall of the Western Empire

The vast Roman Empire was hard to control. In AD 284, Emperor Diocletian (reigned AD 284 to 305) tried to make it easier to look after by splitting it in two – a western half and an eastern half, each with its own emperor. Some fifty years later, Emperor Constantine (reigned AD 307 to 337) chose a town in the east, in present-day Turkey, to be the new capital of the Roman world. He called it Constantinople. The Eastern Empire flourished, but the Western Empire collapsed. Barbarians invaded it and Rome was sacked. The end came in AD 476, when the last emperor of the Western Empire left.

Attila was a leader of the Huns, a tribe that originally came from the east.

A Saxon warrior. Starting in the AD 500s, the Saxons spread from northern Europe into Britain.

Carvings like this showed that the emperors of the Western and Eastern empires had equal importance.

The invading soldiers carried shields, swords, and lances. They wore armor made from scale-like metal plates.

Justinian (reigned from AD 527 to 565), the emperor of the Eastern Empire, tried to regain the Western Empire. He met with some success.

The enemies of Rome

Outside the Roman Empire lived people the Romans described as "barbarians." They were tribes such as Goths, Vandals, Franks, and Saxons. Further away, in central Asia, lived the warlike Huns. When the Huns moved into Europe, they displaced the tribes in their way. Entire communities fled, and refugees sought shelter inside the Roman Empire. At first the Romans tolerated the new arrivals, but then they tried to drive them back. The Romans were no match for the invaders, and they overran the Western Empire.

Emperor Valerian (reigned from AD 253 to 260) tried to regain territory in the Middle East. But he was taken prisoner by the Persian king, Shapur (seen here on the right) and died in captivity.

Visigoth jewelers crafted this bronze and enamel brooch in the shape of an eagle.

Christianity survived the fall of the Western Empire, and the Church grew strong.

Londinium

Paris
Lugdunum
Burdigala • Mediolanum
Tolosa • • Ravenna • Sirmium
Tarraco • Massilia Florentia
Rome • Constantinople
Gades Caralis Neapolis • Thessalonica
Tingis Carthage • Athens • Ephesus • Antioch
Corinthus
Syracuse

Vandals, Sueves
Huns
Ostrogoths
Visigoths
Franks
Angles, Saxons, Jutes
Lombards

Leptis Magna Cyrene Alexandria • Jerusalem
Cairo

The Byzantine Empire
Constantinople was a "new Rome" in the east. It was the capital of the Byzantine Empire – another name for the eastern part of the Roman Empire. For 1,000 years it remained a major Christian city until, in 1453, it fell to the Muslims.

The great 6th century church of Santa Sophia, in Constantinople.

Byzantine churches have their own distinctive style.

The legacy of the Romans
We have inherited much from the Romans. Many modern languages are influenced by Latin; some of our buildings are based on styles used by the Romans; roads still in use in Europe were planned by Roman engineers; and the Catholic Church still has its headquarters in Rome – a link with Roman civilization.

Theodora (right), Justinian's wife, was an able politician. She influenced many of her husband's decisions regarding the Empire.

A glass drinking horn (left) made by a Roman craftsman.

INDEX